We all have stories to tell.

Digital Storytelling

Digital Storytelling

TESOL Strategy Guide

DAVID KENT

Pedagogy Press

National Library of Australia Cataloguing-in-Publication entry:
Kent, David Bradley, author.
Digital storytelling / David Kent.

ISBN: 9781925555004 (paperback)
TESOL strategy guide ; 1.
Includes bibliographical references.
Teachers of English to Speakers of Other Languages.
Digital storytelling—Study and teaching.
English language—Study and teaching—Foreign speakers.
372.6770285

Pedagogy Press. Sydney, Australia.
www.pedagogypress.com

First Edition.

For teachers everywhere.

CONTENTS

	Preface	xi
1	Overview	1
2	What is digital storytelling?	2
3	How can I use digital storytelling?	3
4	What types of digital storytelling exist?	5
5	What elements are behind an effective digital story?	6
6	How can digital storytelling lend itself to TESOL?	10
7	How can I start using digital storytelling with students?	11
8	How do I evaluate a digital story?	13
9	What tools are available for digital storytelling creation?	16
10	How do I craft a digital story?	19
11	How would I use a tool to create a digital story?	26
12	What are the key points behind digital storytelling use in the TESOL context?	50
13	Lesson plan guides, and example implementation	53
14	Photocopiable material	75
15	Resources list	82
16	References	153

Preface

This *TESOL Strategy Guide*, number one in the set, arose out of the clear need to provide teacher training and a means of professional development to educators, living and working in the Republic of Korea. Many expatriate English language instructors have arrived in-country without training as a teacher or educator, and are often left to take care of their own professional development while engaged in teaching English to speakers of other languages (TESOL). As many of these teachers come to enjoy working as expatriates, they often begin to seek out their own professional development on topics that they wish to learn more about, on skills that they wish to gain, and on techniques that they wish to integrate within their classrooms. It is this need, which is common to all teachers of English in all contexts around the globe, that this book seeks to fill.

Organization of the text

Each *TESOL Strategy Guide* can be read standalone or in conjunction with others from the set. Each book provides information on a technology topic, and has been designed around a question-based format similar to the following:

- Overview
- What is ... ?
- How can I use ... ?
- What types of ... exist?
- What elements are behind an effective ... ?
- How can ... lend itself to TESOL?
- How can I start using ... with students?
- How do I evaluate a ... ?
- What tools are available for ... creation?
- How do I craft a ... ?
- How would I use a tool to create a ... ?
- What are the key points behind ... use in the TESOL context?

A comprehensive list of resources with links to pertinent web sites and applications is included, along with lesson plan guides, example implementation techniques, and various free to use handouts for the teacher and student alike. A reference list of all works cited also allows those teachers with an interest in a particular topic to engage in reading further on the issues that most interest them and impact their learners.

It is hoped that this book will provide both education and something new for all teachers – be they trained or untrained, pre-service, in-service, seasoned, or retired.

1

Overview

Digital storytelling clearly stands out as an exciting and captivating approach to use for both the teaching and practice of digital literacy, media literacy, and visual literacy skills. The exciting potential behind its use in the teaching of English to speakers of other languages (TESOL) is its ability to give a voice to those students who might come and sit quietly in class and rarely have a chance to speak. Success with digital stories therefore comes when students are empowered with the ability to talk about and make meaning from their life experiences. This book focuses on the use and applicability of digital storytelling in the TESOL context. Attention is placed on the types and effectiveness of digital storytelling, along with constructive means for evaluating student-produced content. A hands-on look at the digital storytelling process provides a practitioner guide, and this is then reinforced with a variety of useful resources to assist both students and teachers alike in getting started with digital storytelling.

2

What is digital storytelling?

Digital storytelling is the art of combining the skill of storytelling with a mixture of digital graphics, text, audio narration, video, and music (Ohler, 2008), and so the story is therefore primarily a visual one. Digital storytelling scripts are often first person narratives that tell the story in one's own voice and one's own style. As such, each story tends to revolve around a particular theme and contains a single viewpoint that is presented in two to three minutes. The essential challenge that digital storytelling poses to teachers is that of engaging students in the meaningful use of digital imaging (Robin & Pierson, 2005), and seeing students use digital imaging as a mode of communication and for personal reflection (Jenkins & Lonsdale, 2007); in other words, developing learner multimedia literacy levels while guiding students in making meaning from experience.

3

How can I use digital storytelling?

Digital storytelling essentially allows students to practice multimedia literacy skills. As such, educators in all teaching contexts can employ digital storytelling in a multitude of ways, from introducing new material to assist students in learning to conduct research, through to synthesizing large amounts of content and gaining expertise in the use of digital communication and authoring tools. Instructor created digital stories can also be deployed as a lesson hook, a way to integrate multimedia into the curriculum, to assist in making difficult or complex content more easily understood, or to serve as a jump point for facilitating classroom discussion (Robin, 2008). Student created digital stories, on the other hand, can come to assist learners with idea organization as they begin to develop stories for an audience, and present their ideas and knowledge in uniquely meaningful, individual, and personal ways (Bull & Kajder, 2004). Of course, challenges for students can and do arise, and they range from difficulties in formulating a sound argument through to learners holding low interest in storytelling. Aspects of the digital divide may also see some students having limited access to the appropriate hardware and software to work with digital storytelling dissemination and development. Other students may simply not possess adequate multimedia literacy skills to develop a digital story. Further, content creation with digital storytelling can be time-consuming, and students and teachers who embark on this endeavor need to be well versed in educational fair-use policies, along with the copyright and intellectual issues pertaining to digital content creation and dissemination (Robin, 2008).

4

What types of digital storytelling exist?

Robin (2008) identifies several different types of digital storytelling, including:

Personal narratives

These are character stories, stories about significant life events, stories about what we do, or any other kind of personal stories like discovery stories, love stories, and recovery stories.

Historical themes and events

These are more than electronic encyclopedia entries; such stories should aim to become engaging and insightful mini-digital documentaries.

Stories that inform or instruct

All digital stories inform or instruct. However, the distinction for this type of digital story is that it is specifically created to deliver learning content, which can cover all academic fields from maths through to medicine.

5

What elements are behind an effective digital story?

It is important for teachers to assist students in creating digital stories that are effective. The Center for Digital Storytelling (CDS, 2016), along with Lambert (2010), outlines seven key elements that combine to form an effective digital story: point of view, dramatic question, emotional content, economy, pacing, gift of voice, and soundtrack.

Point of view

As digital stories are constructed from students' own experiences and understanding, an embedded point of view in a story comes to successfully establish power of expression for the writer.

Dramatic question

A single dramatic question can serve to hold the attention of the audience throughout the telling of a digital story. However, the question must be answered by the conclusion of the story.

Emotional content

Good stories elicit some kind of emotional response from the audience, like laughter, joy, tears, or surprise. Emotional responses draw an audience in, and allow them to connect to the story.

Economy

Script economy is perhaps one of the most difficult elements of digital storytelling to perform well. Digital stories are concise and are normally two to three minutes in length (about one double-spaced page of text). Particular emphasis on this aspect in educational settings may make the construction process more manageable for learners.

Pacing

Pacing of speech is important. The pausing and varying of speech rhythms are essential to avoid monotony.

Gift of voice

This aspect of digital storytelling, the gift of voice, is one of the most important for language classrooms.

Many teachers have those unheard students who are seen entering, submitting work, and leaving at the sound of the bell, but not participating in discussion, group activities, or any task that asks for their verbal participation. The process of digital storytelling allows these students to record themselves verbally narrating their own scripts, and if they are still too shy to speak, the process uniquely allows them to voice their opinions through text titles, highlighting their opinions and presenting their voice in 'silent movie' style.

An accompanying soundtrack

A well chosen and well timed accompanying soundtrack is extremely important. Music can enhance and underscore aspects of a digital story by adding additional layers of complexity and depth to the narrative.

As a point of note here, Robin (2016) would see these seven elements increased to ten within the educational context, adding aspects such as the use of grammar and language, the overall purpose of the story, and the quality of media elements chosen.

6

How can digital storytelling lend itself to TESOL?

For digital stories to be effective in the TESOL context, it is important that teachers and students focus on different aspects. Teachers can use digital storytelling as a presentation media appealing to diverse learning styles, to generate interest in topics, call attention to a subject, motivate learners, and capitalize on the imaginative talent of students as they start researching and telling their own stories. Students can develop communicative skills by asking questions, expressing opinions, constructing narratives, and writing for an audience. Collaboration of learners in story construction can see summary reports evolve into communication products, with authentic application for the lessons learned in class. Students will also increase their computer skills, and utilize software that combines a variety of media elements including text, still images, audio, and video.

7

How can I start using digital storytelling with students?

The process of digital storytelling assists with developing several language skills such as reading and writing when storyboarding, and speaking and listening during collaboration and narration. It can also assist in enlarging vocabulary. When working in groups, students are able to share ideas, collaborate on picture selection, communicate, and engage in unique authentic experiences that can transform their understanding of text, words, and images.

A number of traditional TESOL classroom tasks and activities can also easily be transferred to the digital storytelling setting, and they involve: retelling, process writing, portfolio development, and even the digitization of the classroom photo wall. Activities that are well-suited to digital storytelling involve movie trailer development, simulated news broadcasts, product advertising commercials, oral history and re-enactment projects, and virtual tours of schools or cities. Essentially, a great number of classroom tasks or activities can be spiced up with a digital storytelling twist, depending upon the willingness, creativity, and imagination of both the teacher and the students.

8

How do I evaluate a digital story?

Perhaps the most appropriate means available to evaluate a digital story, particularly in the TESOL context, is to use a prefabricated rubric based upon a Likert-type rating scale. Any such rubric should be presented to students beforehand, so that they can understand what will be assessed and expected from them.

Evaluation rubrics, particularly those using indicators across several categories, are essential when assessing the quality of student work on any complex multimedia-based project. Although it is useful for the busy teacher to apply pre-made rubrics, it is even better if teachers formulate ones of their own, so that such rubrics can reflect their teaching environment and the points they wish to assess. One good source for this is Rubistar, where there are a number of pre-made evaluation options as well as information on how to create unique context sensitive evaluation instruments. The rubrics section of the resources list also contains several other rubric creation tools that may prove worthwhile to look over.

The rating scale used in the following rubric goes from 1 to 5, with 1 being poor, 2 fair, 3 average, 4 good, and 5 excellent. 'Average' is used as a midpoint so that students can see how each particular skill relates to peers. This allows teachers to identify those skills that are weak in individual students, and those that may need improvement.

Assessment Item	Assessment Criteria	Score
Point of View/Purpose	Establish a purpose early on, and maintain a clear focus throughout.	1 2 3 4 5
Voice/Pacing	Rhythm and voice fit the story line, and help the audience to get into the story.	1 2 3 4 5
Images	Images create a distinct atmosphere and tone, and aid in communicating symbolism and metaphor.	1 2 3 4 5
Economy	The story is told with the right amount of detail throughout – it does not seem too short or too long.	1 2 3 4 5
Language Use	Language use is appropriate, and contributes to the clarity, style, and overall character of the story.	1 2 3 4 5

Ratings: 1 Poor 2 Fair 3 Average 4 Good 5 Excellent

9

What tools are available for digital storytelling creation?

A variety of different software applications are available that provide support for the creation of digital stories, and a number of examples are provided in the digital story creation section of the resources list. Some of these tools are expensive, and others are free. Purely online editing tools have become available as well as app-based tools for Android and iOS devices. The most notable computer-based tools are:

Microsoft Photo Story 3 is a Windows free download that allows for the manipulation of still images and audio using a wizard. It is an easy to use program most suited for young children but also usable with adults.

Windows Live Movie Maker is a Windows free download that allows for the manipulation of still images, video, and audio clips. The software application was previously built into Windows, but is now available separately, and is a more sophisticated application than Photo Story.

Apple iMovie allows for the manipulation of still images, video, and audio clips, and is preloaded with OS X.

Adobe Photoshop Elements is cross-platform compatible with Windows and OS X, allows for the easy modification of images and text slides, and is available in an academic version.

Goldwave is a digital audio editor that provides simple recording as well as more sophisticated processing, restoration, enhancement, and conversion for Windows and Linux. A free version is available for evaluation purposes, after which a lifetime license can be purchased.

In mobile contexts for tablets and smartphones, **WeVideo** is a useful tool for digital story creation. It is a web-based app, an Android-based app, and an iOS-based app. So, it is available across a wide variety of platforms and to many users. It is a free video editor that can mix images, text, video, and audio. Several free templates, with transitions, and corresponding images, effects and themes are available, while some enhanced functionality is only available in a paid upgrade.

10

How do I craft a digital story?

A four stage, step-by-step approach, to the creation of digital stories (based on Robin, 2008) is as follows:

Stage One – Define, collect, decide

- Select a topic for the digital story.
- Search for images (pictures, photographs, charts).
- Locate audio resources (music, speeches, interviews).
- Find informational content (PDF files, Microsoft Word files, Microsoft PowerPoint slides).
- Start thinking about the underlying purpose of the story, and aspects of narrative.

Stage Two – Select, import, create

- Select appropriate still and moving images for use in the story.
- Select appropriate audio as a background track or for sound effects.

- Select the content and text to utilize.
- Import images, video, and audio into the movie making application.
- Modify the number of images, or the image order, and clip audio/video where necessary.

Stage Three – Decide, write, record, finalize

- Decide on the underlying purpose and point of view of the story.
- Write a script to use for narration.
- Record the narration for use in the movie making application.
- Finalize by saving the digital story as a video file.

Stage Four – Demonstrate, evaluate, replicate

- Share the digital story with colleagues.
- Gather feedback on how best to further develop, expand, and implement the digital story in the classroom.
- Run a digital storytelling workshop.

In the TESOL context, however, a different approach is really needed as technology is not always required for these steps – nor is it always available. In this context, there are several steps to undertake when going about developing digital stories with students. Steps one through three can be done with or without a computer, tablet, or access to the use of technology, although steps four to six will, by their nature, require access. The steps that can be completed traditionally may be undertaken during class time with teacher support, or assigned for homework. So too, steps four through six, may be undertaken either in a technologically equipped classroom such as a computer lab, or by students at home if they possess the technological skills and equipment. Most importantly, these steps are a guide to understanding what is necessary for the process of digital storytelling development, and can be adapted for individual use.

Taking all of this into account, and in following the steps outlined by Jakes (2009), the production process might then, in TESOL contexts, follow steps that start with writing, script preparation, storyboarding development, then resource location and digital development prior to sharing.

Step One – Writing

Start students out with a topic or assignment where they will need to prepare no more than a 500 word narration.

Step Two – Script preparation

Work on tightening up the narration, and ensure that the maximum word count is not exceeded.

Step Three – Storyboarding development

To assist students in working collaboratively to lay out their ideas, a storyboarding handout, which may be found in Chapter 14 and photocopied for classroom use, can be provided: one that can be used by students when initially beginning to think about the development of their story, the media artifacts they might wish to include, and what they might wish their story to achieve or communicate. This provides a point from which students can then in turn begin to compose their narrative script, and space on the handout is provided for this purpose. Further, the storyboarding and scripting section of the resources list contains information on several applications that may be used with students when developing and constructing storyboards.

Step Four – Resource location

The next step would be locating the actual media resources that students require (images, music, sounds, and so on), and the resources list at the end of this book contains information on a number of means available for this purpose. This resource location step could be undertaken in the computer lab during class time, but it might prove better to set this task as homework. In a later lesson, students would then need to bring their media resources to the classroom on a USB stick, or access them through an online storage system (such as Dropbox, Google Drive, and so on).

Step Five – Digital development

The next step is that of actually creating the digital story, and this does require the use of a computer lab, or in-class use of tablets. Students would follow the storyboard that they had developed, and apply their media resources appropriately while using software to produce their digital story.

Step Six – Sharing

The final step then involves presentation of the created digital story. The presentation step can be conducted in class to a closed audience of teacher and students, or the digital stories could be shared privately online in a digital video archive such as YouTube.

To complete a digital storytelling activity in TESOL contexts, there are essentially technology-optional and technology-required steps. The technology-optional steps, one through three above, focus on a write, research, rewrite process, where narration leads to storyboarding. The remaining steps are the technology-required, where step four focuses on the location of media artifacts to accompany a developed narration, and steps five and six lead to the finalization, recording and ultimately the sharing of the digital story itself.

11

How would I use a tool to create a digital story?

There are many tools to choose from when deciding to make a digital story. One software-based tool is Photo Story 3, for which a free download is provided by the Microsoft Corporation, with the software working by stepping users through a wizard with each stage being completed in a set sequence. Regardless of the creation tool chosen, good preparation of images and audio (music and narration) is important. In the case of software such as Photo Story 3, or cross-platform options such as WeVideo, these digital story creation tools are very easy to use, especially for younger learners, and allow for the development of multimedia presentations that incorporate digital images, sound, narration, and various visual effects and transitions like zooming, scanning, and fading. However, Photo Story 3 does not process video, so the use of WeVideo or a more complex program such as iMovie or Movie Maker would be required for that purpose if required. So too, if seeking cross-platform flexibility, a web-based app such as WeVideo, which is also available as a native application for Android and iOS devices, would likely prove more suitable in the mobile context, or with older learners such as university students and adults.

A short overview in how to get started in using such tools follows, starting with Photo Story 3 and then moving to WeVideo. Please keep in mind that although tools do at times change the features that they offer, and at times the layout of the interface, or even may become defunct, the following guides have been written in a way that any such changes will not impact on understanding the essential mechanisms for using any of the digital story creation tools to develop a digital story project, and the ultimate publishing, saving, or uploading of it as a movie file.

11A. Using Photo Story 3

Preparation

All digital images, sounds and narration files that students want to use in their project need to be collated and stored in a single directory on the computer. Storing all content in the same folder ensures that all project files can be easily found, and allows for easy perusal of potential digital story content by teachers and students before the movie making process begins.

Step One – Getting started

Open the Photo Story 3 software, and on the first screen select 'Begin a new story' and click 'Next'. You also have the choice here to edit a previously constructed story, or to play a story, from this initial start page.

Step Two – Importing and arranging images

Click 'Import pictures', then browse to the location where the digital story content files are located, and then select the images required to construct the digital story. Holding down the 'shift' key while selecting images will allow students to import a series of multiple files at one time, or a series of individual photos can be chosen by holding down the 'ctrl' key while selecting files to import. More images can be added at a later time by repeating this process. The software will import a wide variety of the most common image file formats (for example, BMP, JPG, PNG, TIF) up to a total of 300 images per movie.

After the selected images are imported, they will appear in the 'Timeline' view which allows students to select each image for editing or reordering. Images can be moved around the 'Timeline' by left-clicking on the image, keeping the mouse button held down, and dragging the image to a new position. Letting the mouse button go places the image in its new position. Images can also be selected one by one for simple editing like cropping and rotating, or by clicking the 'Edit' button to change the brightness, contrast, color, and so on. In addition, a number of effects can be applied to the photos including black and white, color pencil, and sepia. So too, clicking on the 'Remove black borders' option automatically ensures that all images are cropped to fill the screen. At this point, it is wise to click 'Save project' and save the Photo Story 3 project in the digital story folder that was created in the preparation stage. It is important to understand that all editing and saving during the project creation process does not alter the original files. To go to the next step, just click the 'Next' button.

Step Three – Customization:
Titles, effects, motion, transitions, and narration

Titles and texts can be added to any of the imported images by selecting the appropriate image and typing the text in the presented text box. The text can then be aligned to the top, center or bottom of the screen, and presented in various fonts, sizes, and colors. Simple effects can also be added to the images here by clicking 'Add effect', and they are the same as those outlined in the previous step. It might also be worthwhile to create a completely black image to use as a title or credits image at the start or end of the digital story, and it is useful for students to include information such as their names and student numbers in any digital submission. Click 'Next' to go to the following screen where narration can be added and the final files customized further.

In order to customize the movie further, select the image you wish to work with and click 'Customize motion'. You will then be presented with two versions of the selected image showing a 'Start' and 'End' position from which pans and zooms can be set by resizing the boxes that appear overlaid on the images. To zoom in, set the start image box to full size and reduce the size of the end image box. To zoom out, set the boxes in the opposite manner with full size on the end image and reduced on the start image. The duration for the image to appear in the movie can also be set here, but it is recommended that this be left as 'Set duration automatically' or, if it must be changed, be at least three seconds to a maximum of seven seconds. To review the changes just made, and to see if adjustments are required, click the 'Preview' button before clicking 'Save' to save the effect. It is helpful to set the start position to be the same as that of the previous picture so that any transition between images runs smoothly.

To incorporate transitions between images, click on the 'Transitions' tab located at the top of the screen. You will then be presented with the current image and the next image side-by-side with a preview of the transition effect between both of them. Select 'Start current picture using a transition', then choose the desired transition from the list of those available (such as 'Cross-fade'). Set the transition duration to automatic, and then preview the selection. After that, click 'Save' to save the transition before moving on to apply any other desired transitions to the remaining images. After all transitions have been applied click 'Close' to return to the narration editing screen.

To record a narration, first select the image you want to start recording sound over, then click the 'Record sound' button. Speak into the microphone to record the narration, then click the 'Stop' button to finalize recording. Press the 'Preview' button to see how the recording worked out, and if it is acceptable, you can move on; if not, you can repeat the process and record the narration once again. Narration can be recorded over one image at a time or over multiple images at one sitting. Either way, it is advisable to run the 'Sound hardware test' button from this page before attempting to record the first narration. This will ensure the microphone is correctly calibrated, and that the hardware and software are working well together.

Step Four – Background music

The next step is adding background music to the movie, and this can be done by clicking 'Select music' or 'Create music'. A number of music files can be added but it is important that the music be appropriate and preferably an instrumental version so as not to distract from the narration. If selecting 'Create music', you can use a selection of material presented by the Photo Story 3 software which includes the genre of music, the style of music, as well as the bands and moods of the music. The tempo and intensity of the music can also be adjusted, as well as the volume. After making the necessary choices, click on the 'Preview' button to hear how the music will sound. To have different music play over different images, just repeat the process while selecting the various images. After clicking 'OK', the background music then appears as a bar above the 'Timeline' and is automatically adjusted to end with the movie (even if you later decide to delete or add images). Then, click 'Preview' to see how the images and sound work together, and 'Save project' if the results are good or 'Delete music' to start over.

Keep in mind that your script, the recording of your narration, and your personal images belong to you, and that no matter what music you have chosen, even if you have composed it yourself, you should credit the source at the end of your digital story. Unfortunately, many companies today, like YouTube, will automatically block copyright material that you might want to use on a digital story, and this is regardless of the fair use copyright act. However, there are many sites offering copyright and royalty free music that can be used for digital storytelling projects – see the music resources section of the resources list.

Step Five – Publishing the movie file

In this final step, we convert the project file (or WP3 file) into a working movie file which can be exported from Photo Story 3 and saved in a format suitable for submission to the teacher, to send to friends and family, or viewed as part of a portfolio. In this step, a number of publishing options are available from 'Send the story as an email' to 'Save your story for playback on a smartphone', but with each option there is a trade-off in picture quality and file size. Probably the best option to choose for the EFL or ESL teacher and student is the first one, 'Save your story for playback on your computer', then click the 'Browse' button to find the preparation folder (created earlier) as the save location. Follow this up by clicking 'Settings' to alter screen resolution settings if necessary (usually not required), before clicking 'Next'. Movie rendering will then begin, and this can be a lengthy process depending upon the number of images, text titles, and effects, the amount of motion, the length of time between images, the amount of narration, and the size of music files utilized in the project. After this process is complete, click on 'View your story'. The digital story is now complete.

11B. Using WeVideo

Preparation

As with any digital storytelling project, particularly those involving EFL or ESL students, it is best to start out with a clear idea of what digital images, videos, sounds, and narrative script are going to be used to develop the project. This can be achieved by using the handouts at the back of this book, and by following the guidelines for working with students as presented in Chapter 10. Once the digital content and the narrative script has been prepared, WeVideo can be used to easily put together a short digital story using templates and themes, the drag and drop functionality, and with flexibility provided through cross-platform support across multiple devices from computers and tablets through to smartphones. The smartphone and tablet application, as well as the web interface version, have slightly different variations in capability and use, and it is up to the individual teacher as to which version affords the most flexibility and offers the most suitability to their teaching and learning context.

Step One – Getting started

If you are using an iPhone or iPad, you will first need to download the application from the App Store, or from Google Play if running an Android device. If using a computer, you should go to the WeVideo website. The digital story creation section of the resources list has more details regarding these applications and the website. If you are using the smartphone application, you can start to create videos immediately, and for free. These videos are saved locally to your phone, but they will contain a 'WeVideo' watermark in the top right corner, as well as an outro for a few seconds. The watermark is less obtrusive if using a tablet or smartphone for editing, compared to that placed onto videos when finalizing movies using the web interface. If using the website, you will need to first log into your account (or sign up for an account) which can be for personal, business, or educational use. From the web-based interface, projects are saved on the WeVideo server, and finalized movies can be published or saved to various locales such as Facebook, Google Drive, and YouTube.

Step Two – Importing and arranging content

After signing in to the website, you will be able to click 'Create new' in order to open the video editor and to start creating a video project. You also have the choice here to edit a previously constructed story if you have been working with the web-interface previously. However for those using smartphones, the application will launch straight into the video editor on opening. Smartphones have a large '+' button in the bottom right corner that allows you to select videos or photographs from the device. Tablets will offer a drag and drop interface that will allow you to drag media to the timeline, and this is similar to the website interface, which requires each photo or video to first be uploaded by clicking on 'Upload media'.

The photographs or videos can then be sorted into the correct order according to a previously established storyboard developed from a class handout or other in-class projects or homework assignments. Images and video clips can be moved around the 'Timeline' by left-clicking on the image or video clip, keeping the mouse button held down, and dragging to a new position. Letting the mouse button go places the image or video clip in its new position, and the length of time that each image or video is displayed can then be changed. On smartphones and tablets, this can be done by pressing to select the image or video and changing either the duration time of the image and its orientation (portrait or landscape), or by trimming the start or end of the selected video. On the website, each media artifact that has been imported can be individually selected and dragged to the required duration for images, or trim setting for videos.

Step Three – Customization:
Editing attributes, adding effects, motion, and titles
Once the order of images and videos, as well as their durations, has been set, you can start to think about customization. There are several methods of providing customization to a digital story when using WeVideo, and these include being able to add a theme as well as background music, both of which are discussed in the next step. In this step, the focus is on adding captions, animations (for example, scaling,

positioning, fades), transformations (for example, rotation, flipping, fit), and effects (for example, sharpen, sepia, black and white).

Each image or video on the timeline can be selected with a click or a press, after which there are several options for customization. There is a 'Text' button on tablet smartphone devices that allows for captioning and text attribute changes, whereas the website offers an 'Edit' button to access this feature. Captions can then be overlaid on the image or video, and the font, color, and other attributes (such as the duration of the captions being displayed) can then be altered. The image can be pinched to alter the scale and fit, or pressed and moved to alter positioning on tablets and smartphones. These options are also available through the web interface, but they need to be set individually by clicking on the 'Transform' tab, which appears next to the 'Caption' tab when editing an image or video. The 'Transform' tab is also next to an 'Animation' tab that allows for setting of image position (by placement and by scale, and by start and end point), as well as options for fading in and out.

On tablets and smartphones, this option is available after pressing on the image for editing. Videos offer a 'Volume' tab across all interfaces, and this allows for control of the audio level of the clip which may need to be muted in order to allow for background music and narration to later become the focus. There is also a fade in and fade out option for each video clip that has been inserted on the timeline under the 'Volume' tab on the web interface, with the 'Transform' tab offering rotation, flip, fit, scale, and positioning options. A video 'Speed' control tab is also available through the web interface, if using a paid account, and this allows access to fast or slow motion control as well as editing tools such as Chroma key.

Finally, to add a title to the digital story, the first image can be selected and the title changed in a similar manner as adding a caption to an image. Text attributes (such as color, font size and type, and wording) can then be changed as desired. Otherwise, this image can be deleted and you can use an image or video of your choice with a caption overlay as a title. Alternatively, a theme can be selected to provide different start and ending options for the digital story, or one of several freely available backgrounds can be applied if using the web interface.

Step Four – Selecting themes, adding background music, overlaying narration

To work with various themes for a digital story, to add background music, and to overlay a narration, there are three buttons for these purposes. On the web and tablet interfaces, they are located to the left of the storyboard timeline; but on smartphones, they are located above the timeline which is represented vertically (instead of horizontally).

Selecting the 'Theme' button provides a series of free templates that each have their own unique introduction sequences, font formatting, and between image and video transitions for those using the web interface. The level of theme customization is slightly more limited when using the tablet or smartphone application as there are no transition options. Further, the tablet and smartphone interface offers only three free themes while the web interface offers substantially more. After selecting a theme, the web interface automatically inserts the themes transitions between the images and videos on the timeline. To change the type of transition, click on the image representing the transition between images and videos on the timeline. A number of choices from standard cross fades, flips, and wipes are available as well as various patterns like stars and diamond shapes, along with effects like curtains, paper planes, and flares to name a few. Also available through the web interface are various choices of backgrounds that can be used in place of images or videos in the timeline, with various effects and editing options available to customize these backgrounds, and they are similar to those available when working with images and videos. These backgrounds can also be used to end the video or start the video, and they can be used as an alternative to a theme-based ending or introduction sequence. Additionally available from the web interface is a simple text ending image that is similar to the standard text start image that is available across all interfaces. In any case, it is useful for students to include information such as their

names and student numbers as a title on the initial
theme screen, image, or background that is being
used at the start of any project timeline.

Each theme comes with different background music,
and this can be overridden by clicking on the
'Background music' button to the left of the timeline
on tablet devices and for those using the web
interface, or above the timeline on smartphones.
Background music volume levels, particularly if using
your own music over that applied by a theme, needs
to be adjusted so that the narration can be clearly
heard when the digital story is played back, and this
can be done from the background music selection
screen.

If you forego the use of a theme, and would like to
simply add background music to your timeline
project, WeVideo offers a very good selection and
variety of background music from their freely
available archive. The option of being able to select
from a variety of freely available music that is
licensed, so that your video can be made available in
a variety of contexts, means that you can publish your

finalized movie without copyright infringement issues. Alternatively, audio tracks of your own choice can be imported.

The final part of the project, and perhaps the most important one, particularly when engaging in TESOL, is providing the opportunity for students to speak, and in digital stories, this possibility comes in the form of narration. For digital stories, narrations are best prepared in advance so that they can easily be recorded and overlaid onto any intended digital story project timeline. For those using the web interface of WeVideo, there is a microphone button that once clicked gives the option to record the narration while previewing the recording and muting the audio. The narration must be recorded at one time, and in full, so this means a script must be well prepared in advance. Students can then click the 'Microphone' button to record their narration, and watch their movie play as they begin to speak. After recording is stopped, there is an option to adjust the volume of the narration before it is overlaid on the timeline. Those recording audio using their smartphone or tablet device are able to pause the recording as they go, whereas those using the web interface must record the entire narration at once. In either case, the narration can be erased or recorded over as many times as needed, but as previously stated, it must be made in a single recording session before it can be saved as an overlay to the timeline. Once students are happy with their narration, and it matches with the content of their images and video, the project side of digital storytelling creation is complete. All that is left now is to finalize the project as a movie file.

Step 5 – Publishing the movie file

Once all the images and video content have been arranged, and their attributes set accordingly, captions organized, the theme chosen, and any necessary transitions, title text, backgrounds, background music, and narration have been added to the digital storytelling project timeline, and students are happy with the result, the project can then be saved or published as a movie file. In the web interface there is a 'Finish' tab that once clicked, asks for a title for the video, and then provides a number of options for saving or publishing the movie. These options include setting the quality of the video, making the video private or public, and selecting one or multiple destinations. The destination options available via the web interface include: WeVideo, Vimeo, Google Drive, YouTube, Dropbox, Dailymotion, an ftp site, Box, and Facebook. Those using a tablet or smartphone are able to save the file locally, and are then able to send or publish to the location of their choice.

Although there is no time limit to the creation of movies using a tablet or smartphone, the free-to-use web interface does limit the exporting of videos to no more than two minutes per month. This time limit can be useful, as it forces students to be succinct, and to select their content and to word their narrations carefully. In this case, the time limit is displayed in the bottom right hand corner, and as the limit is per month, it allows the application to be used either for short courses or once per term or once per a semester. It should also be noted that digital stories can be created that are longer, but to finalize these as a movie an upgrade to a paid account would need to be secured.

12

What are the key points behind digital storytelling use in the TESOL context?

A number of key points emerge when considering employing the use of digital storytelling in the TESOL context:

- Digital storytelling is a means for both teaching and practicing multimedia literacy.
- Digital storytelling can be tailored to effectively deliver specific content for learning.
- Success with digital storytelling comes solidly from being able to make meaning from experience.
- EFL and ESL students, working with images and text to create a digital story, develop digital literacy, media literacy, and visual literacy skills.
- Adhering to economy can prove to be one of the most difficult elements of the digital story developmental process.
- Evaluating the quality of student digital stories through a rubric allows for both ease of

assessment of complex work, as well as assessing student output across a range of varied indicators across several categories of competency.

- A number of free, easy to use digital storytelling tools exist, and Photo Story 3 and WeVideo are two popular examples.

- The basic steps used to create a digital story are: define, collect, decide; select, import, create; decide, write, record, finalize.

- The digital storytelling production process, in TESOL contexts, consists of: writing, script preparation, storyboarding development, resource location, digital development, and then sharing.

- Digital storytelling does not require technology to complete all steps. In the traditional manner, there are classroom and homework tasks requiring completion prior to any technologically reliant tasks and this establishes a write, research, and rewrite process where narration leads to storyboarding. The location of media artifacts is then made to suit the narration before the finalization, recording, and sharing of the digital story.

- Digital storytelling resources abound, with the internet the best place to locate various resources.

Ultimately, digital storytelling provides a means for those professionals working within the TESOL field an avenue that allows learners under their care to begin to engage with multimedia in a way that provides students with a means to explore their own interests while customizing the learning process and content to their specific learning style, technological skills, and language learning level.

13
Lesson plan guides, and example implementation

Provided here are lesson plan guides, as well as an example of implementation of digital storytelling from a real-world EFL context. The guides are meant to assist in the understanding of how to develop a detailed lesson plan, and to help describe what each component and stage of a lesson may cover. In addition, steps to implement digital storytelling in an after-school program in the Korean context are detailed to demonstrate how digital storytelling has been implemented in practice with fifth-graders in an EFL context over six lessons and a week of class time.

The content covered here includes:
- Lesson plan general guide
- Lesson plan guide for digital storytelling
- Example implementation: Digital storytelling with fifth-graders in Korea

Lesson Plan General Guide	
Teaching Context	
Level of Proficiency and Maturity	Student language level (e.g. beginner, intermediate, advanced). Student age range (e.g. young learners, adults).
Lesson Length	Time allotted for the class (e.g. 35-45 minutes).
Lesson Topic	Major theme or focus of the lesson (e.g. numbers and time).
Objectives	Lesson aims (e.g. to teach students how to tell the time and date accurately).
Outcomes	Learning outcomes (e.g. students will be able to read analog and digital timepieces).
Relevant Prior Learning	Anything that students need to know before starting work on this lesson's content (e.g. students need to have completed Chapter Two of the book, and have previously met language associated with appointments, calendars, and timekeeping).

Teacher Preparation	
Hardware	Types of computer or peripherals required (e.g. USB sticks, MP3 players).
Software	Name of software used (e.g. Photo Story 3, Microsoft Word).
Webpage Links	Hyperlink to web resources (e.g. www.google.com).
Additional Resources	Other necessary materials for the lesson (e.g. handouts, worksheets, textbooks).

Procedure			
Stage and Timing	Objective	Teacher	Students
Review Stage (if required, 5 minutes)	Focus of stage (e.g. encourage the use of previously acquired language).	Indicate what the teacher says and does in each stage of the lesson.	Provide expected examples of student behavior.

Warm-up Stage/Pre-Technology Use (10 minutes)	Focus of stage (e.g. introduce new concepts and language to students in a meaningful manner).	Indicate what the teacher says and does in each stage of the lesson.	Provide expected examples of student behavior.
Main Stage/ Technology-based Activity (20 minutes)	Focus of stage (e.g. allow students to utilize technology to become familiar with and apply the concepts and language content introduced in the lesson).	Indicate what the teacher says and does in each stage of the lesson.	Provide expected examples of student behavior.

Practice Stage (15 minutes)	Focus of stage (e.g. allow learners to utilize the skills and language that they are expected to acquire during the lesson in a practical way).	Indicate what the teacher says and does in each stage of the lesson.	Provide expected examples of student behavior.
Lesson Summation Stage/Post-Technology Activities (10 minutes)	Focus of stage (e.g. instructor reinforces the importance of language concepts and skills acquired, stating how they will be useful in forthcoming lessons).	Indicate what the teacher says and does in each stage of the lesson.	Provide expected examples of student behavior.

Further Considerations	
Follow-Up Activities	Prepare material that can be applied in a follow up class. Also, be ready with activities for students who complete their class work earlier than expected.
Contingency Plan(s)	Always prepare an alternate teaching scenario in case of any problems. For example, a sudden power outage, or a timetabling issue could make the assigned room unavailable.
Evaluation	Reflect on what worked well, and what did not, and how you might deliver the lesson differently or improve upon it when running it again.

Lesson Plan Guide for Digital Storytelling	
Teaching Context	
Level of Proficiency and Maturity	Beginner to advanced. Adaptable for use with young learners through to adults.
Lesson Length	Several lessons (over a week to a term). Homework completion components. Time allotted for each class: 50 minutes.
Lesson Topic	Variable, from movie reviews to other forms of presentation.
Objectives	1. Enhance communication skills by asking questions, expressing opinions, developing narratives, and writing for an audience. 2. Strengthen media literacy and digital literacy skills (use software, images, audio, video, and other media elements or components).
Outcomes	1. Students will create a structured story (beginning, middle, end). 2. Students employ a range of media to tell their story. 3. Students will show evidence of the ability to express personal opinions.
Relevant Prior Learning	Students will need to be familiar with storytelling components.

Teacher Preparation	
Hardware	Computer or tablet, with internet access and microphone, camera, and scanner (if scanning student work). USB sticks or Google Drive for storage.
Software	Photo Story 3, iMovie, or WeVideo. Microsoft Word or Pages.
Webpage Links	Flickr, Google image search, freemusicarchive.org.
Additional Resources	Storyboarding handout for students to complete offline, and to work on in class.

Procedure – Day 1 of 2			
Stage and Timing	**Objective**	**Teacher**	**Students**
Review Stage (10 minutes)	Remind students of storytelling elements. Ask about stories that they like, start to introduce things that students can talk about in a story (such as their pets).	Teacher directs questions about storytelling (e.g. what students did with their pet on the weekend), prompting responses in a storytelling format.	Students briefly tell about their pet or their weekend in story format, using appropriate sequencers.
Warm-up Stage/Pre-Technology Use (15 minutes)	Introduce the digital storytelling concept.	Play students some appropriate examples from YouTube. Brainstorm story ideas.	Students watch a few examples with a lead to brainstorming ideas.

Main Stage (15 minutes)	Drafting a story can be done on a computer or tablet, or on paper with the handout provided in this book. The focus here is on producing the script for narration.	Assist students on working with the language they need to write their draft, and with the completion of their storyboard.	Students can work together on their story, or they may work individually on their draft to determine the text and sequence.
Lesson Summation Stage/Post-Technology Activities (10 minutes)	Students should be reminded of the lessons goals. The story should have been written by this point, and if not, it can be set for homework completion.	Remind students of what they should have achieved, and ask them to gather music and images for homework.	Students should have completed scripts for narration. Homework will be gathering images and music to match the narration.

Procedure – Day 2 of 2			
Stage and Timing	**Objective**	**Teacher**	**Students**
Review Stage (10 minutes)	Remind students of their homework, and check that it has been completed. Ask students to prepare their materials for digitization.	Teacher directs students to prepare their materials for digitization (this includes images, narrative script/audio, and so on).	Students copy their material from a USB stick, or download it to a computer, tablet or smartphone for sequencing.
Warm-up Stage/Pre-Technology Use (10 minutes)	Materials check, and application preparation.	Ensure student materials match their storyboards, and students are ready to create digital stories using the chosen application.	Students ready themselves to record their narration and to sequence their story using the appropriate application and content.

Main Stage (20 minutes)	Students use a digital story application to sequence their images, titles, and themes, and then record their narrative script in the target language.	Assists students in working on the development of their digital story project, and in the recording of their narrative.	Students successfully sequence their story, and record an appropriate narrative with teacher guidance.
Lesson Summation Stage/Post-Technology Activities (10 minutes)	Students should be able to save their digital storytelling project, and produce a movie file ready for playback. Otherwise, they will need to complete the task for homework.	Ensures students have successfully saved a digital storytelling project file, and are able to produce a movie file for playback by the end of the class period (or are able to do so for homework).	Students complete their digital storytelling project, and produce a movie file that they can share with peers and other stakeholders (such as parents).

Further Considerations	
Follow-Up Activities	Students can show their movie to peers in the following lesson. This can allow for listening practice, and provide a means to stimulate class cohesion as students gain insight into the language level of their peers as well as their thoughts and interests.
Contingency Plan(s)	The next lesson in the course syllabus should be ready in case there is a problem with using the digital story creation application. Alternatively, some language games can be prepared to fill in the time if technological problems occur. Several activity sheets for review of previous material should be prepared to allow those students who complete their recording to keep busy with language content.
Evaluation	What are the biggest frustrations for implementation? Can these be remedied next time? What are the successes of the lesson? What did students get out of this activity? Can more language practice be provided?

Example Implementation:
Digital Storytelling with Fifth-Graders in Korea

The Teaching and Learning Context

This example centers on an elementary school English club after school activity program, where classes met every Monday to Friday, and every second Saturday, for 40 minutes each time. Teachers were expected to assist students in practicing their language skills, and as there were no exams, they were free to use any resources that they wished. Student language proficiency was ranked as pre-beginner to pre-intermediate according to school conducted level tests. There were twenty students, twelve boys and eight girls, aged 10 to 11, participating in the program. Digital storytelling implementation occurred over six class periods.

Teaching Material

The teaching material can be broken down into three: the software, the hardware, and the book providing learning content.

The software

Microsoft Photo Story (Version 3) was selected and used because

> it is free of charge,
>
> it uses a simple wizard to create stories, and
>
> it is very user-friendly (especially for young children).

The hardware

Digitizing tools, such as a scanner and microphone, needed to be readily available so that students could record their narrations, and scan their activity sheets.

Learning content

The sing-along book *Brown Bear, Brown Bear, What do you See?* By Martin & Cale was chosen for pedagogical value, authenticity, and resource availability (such as downloadable coloring activity worksheets). Its rhythmic patterns are helpful and engaging for children on the verge of reading, and it provides just the kind of content that fifth graders can easily manipulate and transfer to a digital storytelling context.

Procedure

Digital storytelling was introduced and implemented with students over a one-week period involving six classes that were held Monday to Saturday and running for 40 minutes each time, thereby providing a total of 240 minutes (four hours) of instruction.

Lesson one – Introducing linguistic content

Overview: Using the Brown Bear text, students were able to become familiar with animal and color vocabulary.

Process: The first class lesson introduced the students to the storybook *Brown Bear, Brown Bear, What Do You See?* and familiarized the class with the linguistic content of the text. This involved introducing students to vocabulary associated with animals and colors. After this, the sing-along storybook was held up for students to see while the instructor read the text, reiterating the animal and color vocabulary in the L1 (first language) where necessary. Follow-up activities involved having students read aloud from a copy of the book, with assistance from the teacher, before progressing to the stage where they were able to read the book aloud on their own.

Lesson two – Introducing a digital version of the text

Overview: Introducing a digital version of the text, as sung by the author of the book and found on YouTube, served to provide review for students.

Process: The second lesson involved presenting a version of the original text as a digital story. This digital story was created by the teacher using a mixture of real animal pictures as well as scanned pictures from the downloadable content available for the book, and this was matched to the text as sung by the author. This step digitizes the initial aspects of the preceding lesson, and provides a 'technology warm-up' activity for students. Students were expected to watch the digital story, and listen to the song. The teacher then reintroduced the animal and color vocabulary, and the digital story was played until all students were able to sing along with the original author of the book as the story progressed.

Lesson three – Solidifying target language vocabulary
Overview: Downloadable coloring activity sheets were provided to students, which also offered color and animal vocabulary practice with cloze exercises.

Process: The third lesson aimed to assist the students in solidifying their knowledge of animal and color vocabulary in English through the use of follow-up coloring activity sheets that were printed from the book website, and were used in the digital story presented in the preceding lesson. As students colored and labeled the black and white pictures of animals from the book, the teacher monitored spelling and vocabulary use, and asked several questions of individuals that involved recall checks (such as "What color is the bear?"), and comprehension checks (such as "What animal is that?"). Students were also encouraged with further vocabulary after prompting with questions (such as "What sound does the animal make?"), and to encourage students in producing English as they worked, the song was played and sung throughout the lesson. It was expected that students would, with teacher assistance, complete the printed activity sheets to a certain standard by the end of the class period, as this material needed to be scanned for use in the following class session.

Lesson four – Whole-class digital storytelling development

Overview: Original content from the sing-along book was used as a retelling task, and as an example of what students would need to create for themselves. The final product was then uploaded to the class website.

Process: The fourth lesson involved the actual introduction and student development of a digital story based on the original sing-along book. For this step, students were able to select and order the scanned activity sheets that they had colored and labeled in the previous lesson so that they matched the order of the song as sung by the book's author. This retelling task was a whole group activity that was completed as students sang the song from memory, prompted as necessary by the teacher. After the correct picture order was achieved, images were imported into the Photo Story 3 program and timed to display with the appropriate song lyrics. The teacher explained the digital storytelling development procedure in a step-by-step fashion, before uploading the story to the class website and informing the students that they would be using the program to create their own story in the following lesson. After uploading the produced digital story to the class website, students reviewed the video and sang along with it.

Lesson five – Practice and reinforcement

Overview: Practice and reinforcement came in the form of students producing a sequenced whole-class digital story that used their own drawings of animals which were labeled and colored accordingly. The final product was also uploaded to the class website before being watched by the class as a whole.

Process: The fifth lesson involved students working on construction of original content for a whole-class produced digital story. They had to draw a picture of an animal different to the animals introduced by the book, label the animal and color it appropriately. They also had to introduce their next classmate's picture in a decided sequence. The instructor monitored this work, assisting as required, and helped each student scan their completed activity sheet. As their activity sheets were scanned, the students read and recorded the text of their labeled image for use as part of the audio portion for the digital story narrative. After all images were scanned and sequenced, and the narrative for each animal recorded, children worked with the practitioner in using Photo Story 3 to solidify their digital storytelling creation knowledge for the next class period. This newly created original digital story was then uploaded to the class website, and watched by the class while reviewing new vocabulary.

Lesson six – Follow-up and individual digital story creation

Overview: Students were expected to create individual digital stories entirely by themselves. At the end of the lesson, each digital story was uploaded to the class website to share with parents and peers before being watched together as a class.

Process: In the final lesson, as a follow-up step, students were expected to develop a complete digital story entirely by themselves. This involved drawing, coloring, and labeling several activity sheets to form a scanned sequence, recording matching audio narration, and using Photo Story 3 to produce content in a movie-file format that could be then published on the class website. Throughout this process, the teacher supported the students as they worked, providing technical and linguistic assistance and encouragement as required. At the end of the lesson, each of these digital stories was uploaded to the class website to share with parents and peers before being watched together as a class.

14
Photocopiable material

This section of the book contains all the photocopiable handouts mentioned throughout the text. You can feel free to make as many copies as you require for teaching purposes and for use within your classes. Any other use or distribution should include a citation to the source of the content.

Providing students with a handout to use during storyboarding will help guide them in the development of their narration, as well as the media resources that they ultimately wish to select to accompany it. An example has been provided here. This also allows students to work on their digital story without being tied to the use of technology. Also provided is a lesson plan template that can be used for considering how best to integrate the steps for using digital storytelling with your classes. As such, the template is meant to act as means to begin thinking about how to implement, with your classes, aspects of what has been discovered through this book. The template should be supplemented with any necessary material, along with the staging as well as other aspects of the lesson being adjusted as required.

The following photocopiable material is available:
- Digital storytelling storyboarding resource notes
- Digital storytelling storyboarding handout
- Lesson plan template

Digital Storytelling
Storyboarding Resource Notes

Digital Story Title	Group Members
A title is chosen by students, and written here.	Student names are listed here.

Image	Description	Media Resources
Students sketch an example image (or paste one) here that reflects what will appear at this point in their digital story.	Students will answer one or all of the following questions here: 1. What will your audience see? 2. What will your viewers hear? 3. What are you trying to communicate or achieve?	Students list all of the media they will need in order to construct this part of their digital story. This will help them later search for the right material. They will need to consider: 1. Music, songs, sound effects, voice recordings 2. Photo/video, images, diagrams 3. Text, titles, transitions, motion

Narration

Students will write their accompanying narration here.

Digital Storytelling
Storyboarding Handout

Digital Story Title	Group Members

Image	Description	Media Resources

Narration

Lesson Plan Template

Teaching Context	
Level of Proficiency and Maturity	
Lesson Length	
Lesson Topic	
Objectives	
Outcomes	
Relevant Prior Learning	
Teacher Preparation	
Hardware	
Software	
Webpage Links	
Additional Resources	

Procedure			
Stage and Timing	Objective	Teacher	Students
Review Stage (if required)			
Warm-up Stage/Pre-Technology Use			
Main Stage/ Technology-based Activity			
Practice Stage			
Lesson Summation Stage/Post-Technology Activities			

Further Considerations	
Follow-Up Activities	
Contingency Plan(s)	
Evaluation	

15

Resources list

As sites continuously go down, merge, and emerge, perhaps only a small selection of all appropriate resource content should be presented here. An attempt at keeping the number of resources to a select few for each type also provides a sample that is both comprehensive and extensive, but not overwhelming. Like any other instructor resource list, individuals will be able to add to the content as they find material that is useful, creating their own bookmark list, and over time, come to curate a vast resource library tailored to their individual teaching and learning context. Each section of this list is broken down into applications that are mostly all freely available for use with Android or iOS devices, computers, or web-based platforms.

Teachers who wish to make notes, or to record any additional resources that they come across, can use the notes section at the end of this chapter.

The following content is covered:

- App creation
- Audio creation/editing
- Blogs
- Bookmarking
- Books
- Coding
- Comic strip generators
- Copyright
- Digital story creation
- Image resources
- Image editing
- Interactive whiteboards
- Mashups
- Media timelines
- Music resources
- Podcasting
- Podcatchers
- Presentations
- Publishing
- QR codes
- Rubrics
- Screencasting
- Storyboarding and scripting
- Story creation apps
- Video editing
- Video resources
- WebQuests
- Wikis

App Creation

Android – n/a

iOS – n/a

Computer – n/a

Web

Android Creator [free/paid] creates free Android apps without the need for programming knowledge.

AppMakr [free/paid] is a template based application creator that relies on drag and drop of elements for the development of no-coding required applications. It is available in a variety of languages.

Appy Pie [free/paid] relies on templates as well as drag and drop for users to begin creating their app. It requires no coding skills.

AppYourself [paid] is an app creation tool aimed at the business market.

Como DIY [paid] is a do-it-yourself app creation tool aimed to mostly target to businesses, and is available in a number of languages.

iBuildApp [paid] is a template driven app creator for iPhone and Android phones.

Audio Creation/Editing

Android

PCM Recorder [free] is a simple voice recorder.

Pocket WavePad [free] records edits and adds effects to audio.

TapeMachine [paid] is a graphical sound recorder and editor.

iOS

Pocket WavePad [free] records edits and adds effects to audio.

Voice Memos [paid] is voice recorder that allows multitasking.

Computer

Audacity [free] is an open source digital editing program available for Mac and PC which you can use to record, edit and mix narration and music.

Pocket WavePad [free] records, edits, and adds effects to audio for Mac.

GoldWave [free/paid] is a digital audio editor that provides simple recording as well as more sophisticated processing, restoration, enhancement, and conversion for Windows and Linux. A free version is available for evaluation purposes, after which a lifetime license can be purchased.

Web

Twistedwave [free] is a browser-based audio editor that can record or edit any audio file.

Blogs
Android

Blogaway [free] is a simple application to allow blogging on-the-go. It works with Blogger and allows for post creation, adding of photos, videos, multiple account management, saving of drafts, bookmarking, and a host of formatting options.

iOS

Disqus [free] is a commenting system that can be included in blogs as an add-on. The application provides an easy way to moderate comments and publish responses to keep engagement levels high.

TravelPod – Travel Blog [free] is a blogging application that works on- and offline, and is designed to be used while traveling.

Computer – n/a
Web

Blogger.com [free] will host your blog for free, and aside from being very easy to use, it allows some level of privacy so it can be suitable for use as a class blogging site. From a single account, you can create as many blogs as you wish and determine who is allowed to comment on the content.

BuzzSumo [paid] allows users to search for blog posts that have been highly shared across social media.

Edublogs.org [free] allows teachers to create and mange their own and students' websites. There is room for customization of design and the ability to add various media to this private and secure platform.

Kidblog.org [free] is an easy-to-use, safe, and secure publishing platform designed for students in grades K-12. There are a number of excellent features including privacy and password protection, and there is no need for student personal information to be collected, nor is there any advertising. It is free for up to fifty students per class.

WordPress.org [free] is one of the most popular blogging platforms in use today as it is open-source and is easily customizable. The downloadable software for self-hosting purposes is much more flexible than that available on the blogging platform.

Twitter [free] deserves a mention here as it is useful for microblogging (posting short frequent updates). It allows users to post and read short 140-character posts called 'tweets'.

Tumblr [free] is a blogging platform open to those over thirteen years of age, with most users using pen names over their real names when blogging. Users can post on their blog, follow others, and search posts. It is unique in that posts are divided into media types: text, photo, quote, link, chat, audio, and video.

Bookmarking

Android

Bookmark [free] is a cross-platform app that allows for the syncing of bookmarks across different browsers and devices.

Delicious [free] provides users with the ability to organize links to content on the internet that they would like to save, the ability to discover links, edit tags and comments, and also to explore content saved by friends.

Facebook Save [free] is a built-in option for saving Facebook news content to read at a later date.

Instapaper [free] provides an offline archiving solution for web pages, and it presents this content to be read in newspaper fashion. Content can be highlighted, and notes can be added while reading.

Pinterest [free] allows users to pin posts (for example, web pages, images, and videos) and organize them around a common theme.

Pocket [free] integrates with a large number of third party applications that allow for the building of bookmarks. Web pages, videos, images, and whatever else can be used offline for bookmarking. Archiving maintains the links but removes the content from offline availability.

iOS

Delicious [free] allows users to save content from the internet (including web pages, blog posts, tweets, pictures, and video), and provides options for searching through others' collections of links.

Facebook Save [free] is a built-in option for saving Facebook news content to read at a later date.

Instapaper [free] provides an offline archiving solution for web pages and presents this content to be read in newspaper fashion. Content can be highlighted, and notes can be added while reading.

Pinterest [free] allows users to pin posts (for example, web pages, images, and videos) and organize them around a common theme.

Pocket [free] integrates with a large number of third party applications that allow for the building of bookmarks. Web pages, videos, images, and whatever else can be used offline for bookmarking. Archiving maintains the links but removes the content from offline availability.

Computer

EdwinSoft's UltimateDemon [paid] is link building software that helps to provide search engine optimization to a website.

Pinterest [free] allows users to pin posts (for example, web pages, images, and videos) and organize them around a common theme.

Pocket [free] integrates with a large number of third party applications that allow for the building of bookmarks. Web pages, videos, images, and whatever else can be used offline for bookmarking. Archiving maintains the links but removes the content from offline availability.

ReadKit [trial/paid] offers an Apple Mac curative and archiving platform for the content found in your other bookmarking applications (like Pocket and Instapaper) and RSS readers, and provides an extra level of organization to this content.

Web

Delicious [free] is a social bookmarking site that allows users to bookmark webpages to the internet instead of locally.

Facebook Save [free] is a built-in option for saving Facebook news content to read at a later date.

Instapaper [free] provides an offline archiving solution for web pages, and it presents this content to be read in newspaper fashion. Content can be highlighted, and notes can be added while reading.

OnlyWire [paid] works with WordPress and offers automatic submission of content to social networking and social bookmarking sites.

Pocket [free] integrates with a large number of third party applications that allow for the building of bookmarks. Web pages, videos, images, and whatever else can be used offline for bookmarking. Archiving maintains the links but removes the content from offline availability.

Books

Android

    Wattpad Free Books [free] provides access to free stories and books written by aspiring authors.

iOS

    Free Books – Ultimate Classics Library [free] features free access to 23,469 classic books.

Computer – n/a

Web

    BookRix [free] allows access to thousands of books to read either online or to download as ebooks.

    Children's Storybooks Online [free] provides a series of illustrated stories for all ages to read.

Coding

Android

Run Marco! [free] offers users the opportunity to play an adventure game while they learn to code. The application presents instructions using 'Blocky', which is the same as that used by the official Hour of Code tutorials.

Tynker [free] is an easy way for children to learn programming skills as they solve puzzles to learn concepts and build games, or control robots and drones. A number of templates are available for free.

iOS

Codea [paid] is a software development tool that uses the Lua programming language to teach users how to program.

Hopscotch [free] is an application that allows users to begin learning to code by making games similar to Angry Birds, and sharing them so others can play them.

ScratchJr [free] allows users to program their own interactive stories and games by snapping together graphical programming blocks. The application was inspired by the Scratch programming language.

Tynker [free] is an easy way for children to learn programming skills as they solve puzzles to learn concepts and build games, or control robots and drones. A number of templates are available for free.

Computer

Scratch [free] allows users to create stories, games, and animations using the Scratch programming language, and then share these with others. It is a project of the Lifelong Kindergarten Group at the MIT Media Lab.

Lightbot – Programming Puzzles [paid] is an OS X game-based application that allows players to use programming logic to solve levels. The app is also available for Android and iOS devices.

Web – n/a

Comic Strip Generators

Android

Comic Maker [free] creates comics from the photo gallery.

Comic Strip It! Lite [free] takes photos or use photo gallery images to create a comic.

iOS

Comic Life 3 [paid] turns photos into comic pages, or creates an entire comic from scratch using templates to build pages with speech balloons, comic lettering, and photo filters.

ToonTastic [free] is a wizard-based animated comic or cartoon creator.

Strip Designer [paid] is software for comic creation that uses camera, library, or Facebook photo options to create a comic.

Computer

Comic Creator [paid] is a basic template driven comic creator for use on a Windows computer.

Web

Pixton [free/paid] is an easy to use comprehensive online comic creator that supports narration, and offers a range of signup options from a free fun option to paid educator/business accounts.

MakeBeliefsComix [free] is a basic comic creator that uses black and white images over a four-panel comic strip. An iOS version is also available.

Toonlet [free] allows for anyone to create their own cartoon characters and web comics.

Toondoo [free] allows for the drag and drop creation of comic strips. An iOS version is also available.

Copyright

Android – n/a

iOS – n/a

Computer – n/a

Web

> *Creative Commons Licenses* [free] gives detailed information regarding the various types of licensing afforded to creative commons, and the permissions that each license grants for the specific works.

> *Image Codr* [free] can assist learners and teachers alike in determining how a Flickr image can be used (as determined by the original photographer), and provides users with an automatically generated Creative Commons citation regarding the images use within digital projects.

Digital Story Creation

Android

Com-Phone Story Maker [free] combines audio, photos, and text to create stories while allowing for three different layers of audio.

WeVideo [free] is a web-based video editor that can mix images, text, video, and audio.

iOS

30hands [free] creates a story by adding narration to photos.

Magisto [free] uses a wizard to create a short video based on provided images or video content.

Splice [free/paid] combines photos, videos, music and narrations. Effects and transitions can be added.

WeVideo [free] is a web-based video editor that can mix images, text, video, and audio.

Computer

iMovie [paid] provides video creation and editing software that can create easily shareable content on a Mac. An iOS version is available.

Microsoft Photo Story 3 [free] for Windows lets you create slideshows from a wizard that includes audio, narration, and images.

Windows Movie Maker [free] for Windows operating systems is a video editing software application that allows for narration, audio, images, and video to be mixed and edited, and it comes with transitions and special effects.

Web

Animoto [paid] allows users to submit songs, choose a theme, add their photos, videos, and text to create a digital story that they can share.

Meograph [free] is a digital storytelling tool that relies on Google Earth to create map-based and timeline-based narrated stories.

WeVideo [free] is a web-based video editor that can mix images, text, video, and audio.

Image Resources

Android – n/a

iOS – n/a

Computer – n/a

Web

Cagle Cartoons [free] provides access to a number of political cartoons from around the world. The images are organized by topic with artists categorized by country.

Flickr Creative Commons [free] provides images that can be used for almost any educational project, as long as proper citation is followed

FreeFoto.com [free] has a photos area that is available under three licensing options: recognition, Creative Commons, and commercial.

Morguefile [free] provides a range of images that are copyright free, and are available for use with few or no restrictions.

Pics4Learning.com [free] is a website that provides safe and free images for educational uses. Images here are copyright-friendly and can be used for classrooms, multimedia projects, websites, videos, portfolios, or other projects.

PicSearch [free] allows you to search the internet for images, but be aware that the image may not be copyright-free, or that it may require permission to be used in projects or in any other educational contexts.

The Library of Congress Prints & Photographs Online Catalog [free] makes an attempt to ensure that as many of their images as possible are available online in a digital format.

Wikimedia [free] serves as a point from where all the images and video posted in Wikipedia can be viewed. Most of the images found here are either copyright-free or free for use with minimal restrictions.

Image Editing

Android

PicSay [free] can edit photos, overlay titles, and add special effects.

FX Camera [free] is a photo booth app that allows users to add various effects to photographs.

iOS

PhotoPad [free] can create, edit, and save vector illustrations. It can also work with photo library images.

ScreenChomp [free] allows you to share, explain, and markup images.

Computer

PhotoPad [paid] is an image editor for OS X.

PaintShop Pro [paid] is a comprehensive image editing package for Windows.

Web

Adobe Photoshop CC [paid] is a comprehensive cloud-based image editing package.

Phixr [free] is an online photo editor with various filters and effects, and it can connect to various social media sites.

FotoFlexer [free] is an online image editor offering a number of effects, distortions, and other features.

Pixlr [paid] is a comprehensive online photo editing app.

Interactive Whiteboards

Android

ExplainEverything [free] allows users to share their content by using an interactive screencasting whiteboard.

Interactive Whiteboard [free] is a virtual whiteboard that can be used for drawing or teaching various concepts as it allows for multiple finger input, straight line drawing mode, drawing move mode, and various other features.

PPT and Whiteboard Sharing [free] provides a way to share presentations, videos, and drawings in various settings including the classroom, the boardroom, and online meetings.

Whiteboard: Collaborative Draw [free] is a collaborative drawing application that allows real-time painting.

iOS

Doceri [trial/paid] combines screencasting, desktop control, and an interactive whiteboard in one application, with control through Airplay or through Mac or PC.

Educreations Interactive Whiteboard [free] is an interactive whiteboard and screencasting tool that allows annotation, animation, and narration of a number of content types.

Screenchomp [free] allows users to annotate pictures or to use the application as a whiteboard. Any work completed with the application can be saved automatically to the internet.

ShowMe Interactive Whiteboard [free] allows voice-over recording of whiteboard interactions so that tutorials can be created easily before being shared online.

Computer

Open Sakore [free] is open-source and it is dedicated to teacher and student use. It allows for insertion of multiple document types, along with annotation capabilities for commenting drawing and highlighting content.

Smoothboard Air [free] is a collaborative interactive whiteboard for multiple iPads and for Android tablets. It allows users to annotate desktop applications wirelessly through the use of a web browser.

Web

A Web Whiteboard [free] is a online whiteboard application that allows a number of devices (like computers, tablets, and smartphones), to draw sketches, and to collaborate with others around the globe.

Realtime Board [free] is a whiteboard in a browser that allows for collaboration among a number of users.

Twiddla [free] is a web-based meeting environment that allows users to mark up photos, graphics, and websites, or to just start out with a blank canvas.

Web Whiteboard [free] is a simple way to draw and write together online by creating an online whiteboard with a click, and sharing it live or by sending the link to others.

Mashups

Android

Edjing 5 DJ Music Mixer [free] not only transforms any android device into a turntable, but it provides access to a range of music libraries.

iOS

iMashup [paid] is a professional quality remixing app that allows users to create their own mashups and remixes.

Pacemaker [free] allows users to create and save mixes on an iPhone or iWatch, and to DJ live from iPad devices.

Computer

Mixxx [free] is an advanced open source DJ package that includes an extensive array of features for OS X and Windows.

Web

Mashstix [free] is a website with user submitted mashups available.

Media Timelines

Android

> *RWT Timelines* [free] allows students to create a graphical representation of any event or process by displaying items sequentially along a line. The final product can be exported as a pdf, or saved to the device's camera roll.

> *Timeline* [free] allows users to create timelines and associate them with colors, and to view multiple timelines together. It is a useful reference tool for remembering dates.

iOS

> *TimelineBuilder* [paid] allows users to create custom timelines with images and text with unique beginning and end dates.

> *Timeline Maker* [free] provides an easy way to display a series of events in a chronological order.

Computer

> *Edraw Timeline Maker* [paid] is a tool that makes it simple to create a professional looking timeline, history, schedule, time table, or project plan diagram from scratch.

TimelineMaker [paid] provides a simplified timeline charting tool aimed at project planners, and business professionals, and those in educational contexts.

Web

Capzles [free] allows users to create rich multimedia experiences from videos, photos, music, blogs, and documents by integrating these into a timeline of sequential events, and then share them on various social media platforms.

Hstry [free] is specifically designed for the education sector, and it allows teachers and students to create interactive timelines for assignments and online sharing.

OurStory [free] offers a means for creating story-based timelines with pictures.

Timeline [free] from *readwritethink* allows students of all ages to easily create a graphical representation of related items or events in sequential order and display them along a line using various images and text.

TimeGlider [free] is a web-based timeline project creator that allows zooming and panning across timelines. Users are able to set the size of events as they relate to importance.

Tiki-Toki [free/paid] is a web-based timeline editor that allows viewing of timelines in 3D, and it allows for the integration of images and videos.

WhenInTime [free] is a web application for creating and sharing media-based timelines.

Music Resources

Android

FindSounds [free] can be used to search the internet for sounds that can then be saved as ringtones, notifications, or alarms.

Shazam [free] allows Android device users to identify the music playing around them, as well as discover song lyrics, and other music related information and tracks.

iOS

Shazam [free] allows iOS device users to identify the music playing around them, as well as discover song lyrics, and other music related information and tracks.

Computer – n/a

Web

300 Monks [free] provides a comprehensive source of royalty free music.

ccMixter [free] is a free music site that is community based and promotes a remix culture. *A cappella* and remix tracks licensed under Creative Commons are available for download and use in creative works.

FMA (Free Music Archive) [free] provides access to a range of free music based on a wide variety of genre. The music is offered free under various licenses for use.

Find Sounds [free] is a long-running service that can be used to search the internet for various sounds that can then be incorporated into various projects.

FreePlay Music [free] is a service that searches the internet for free music that can be used in YouTube videos and other projects.

Podcasting

Android

Podomatic Podcast & Mix Player [free] provides access to a wide variety of podcasts, listening in offline mode, and features such as a dynamic social feed so you can see the podcasts Facebook friends follow and like.

iOS

PodOmatic Podcast Player [free] provides access to a wide variety of podcasts, listening in offline mode, and features such as a dynamic social feed so you can see the podcasts Facebook friends follow and like.

Computer

Audacity [free] is a free multi-track audio recorder and editor with some very powerful features that include those for adding effects to files and conducting analysis of the audio recorded.

iTunes [free] offers media on demand and a way to organize and enjoy music, movies, and TV shows, as well as accessing and subscribing to podcasts and screencasts.

LoudBlog [free] is a Content Management System (CMS) for podcasts. This program automatically generates skinnable websites and RSS-feeds for audio and video podcasts, including provision for show notes and links.

PodcastGenerator [free] is an open source content management system for podcast publishing. It provides a comprehensive range of tools to manage all aspects of podcast publishing.

PodProducer [free] allows for the recording of voice and the adding of effects.

Web

ESLPod [free] provides a range of podcast content tailored to second-language learners of English from specific topics through to test-taking guides.

FeedForAll [free] allows for the creation, editing, and publishing of RSS feeds.

Feedity [free] is an online tool for creating an RSS feed for any web page, with an option to upgrade to a premium account that offers additional features.

FETCHRSS: RSS Generator [free] is an online RSS feed generator, that can create a feed out of almost any web page, automatically updates the RSS feed when new content is added to the web page, and generates an RSS for a social networking site.

OPML Viewer [free] allows users to view the contents of outline processor markup language (OPML) files.

Podcast Alley [free] is the place to go if you are interested in podcasts, want to gain access to the top podcasts, and want to find out the latest news about podcasts.

Pod Gallery [free] is a podcasting website where podcasters can share their episodes, and where listeners can subscribe.

QT-ESL Podcasts [free] provides a range of podcasts that cover oral grammar practice and includes scripts and worksheets.

SoundCloud [free] is a social sound platform where anyone is able to create and share audio.

Podcatchers

Android

Podcast Player [free] provides a range of podcast discovery options and tools, along with a range of features including a sleep timer, video support, intelligent silence skip and volume boost, as well as support for tablet, Chromecast, and Android Wear.

Podcast Republic [free] is an application that is ad-supported. It offers a variety of features from podcast discovery and automatic downloading through to storage management, sleep timer, and car mode. Support is also included from Chromecast and Android Wear.

Pocket Casts [paid] shows subscribed podcasts in a tile format, with easy sorting and categorization functions. Video podcast is also supported, along with auto-download and cleanup of downloaded and played episodes to save on storage space. Several features allow it to stand out, including a sleep timer as well as its cross-platform nature that grants it the ability to sync between multiple devices and mobile operating systems.

iOS

Overcast: Podcast Player [free] provides a combination of powerful audio and podcast management features. The application comes with a wide variety of features that allow it to download episodes, send notifications of new episodes, and play content offline or by streaming. It can also normalize speech levels, and speed through gaps and silence in podcasts.

Castro: High Fidelty Podcasts [free] is a simple and easy to use podcatcher. It provides a simple design with automatic episode download, dynamic storage management, along with episode streaming.

Pocket Casts [paid] shows subscribed podcasts in a tile format, with easy sorting and categorization functions. Video podcast is also supported, along with auto-download and cleanup of downloaded and played episodes to save on storage space. Several features allow it to stand out, including a sleep timer as well as its cross-platform nature that grants it the ability to sync between multiple devices and mobile operating systems.

Computer

gPodder [free] is an open source media aggregator and podcast client. It is able to store information in the cloud on which shows you have listened to, and it allows for the local installation of the client for download of content.

iTunes [free] is a comprehensive media aggregator that provides comprehensive support for media management, the audio and video playback of local media, podcast search and subscription, along with automatic downloads, syncing and streaming, and many other features.

Juice [free] is a long-standing cross platform no-frills podcast aggregator that is open source, and specifically designed to manage podcasts. Features include auto cleanup, centralized feed management, and for Windows users, accessibility options for the blind and visually impaired.

Web

Cloud Caster [free] is a web-based podcaster which works across all mobile devices. It syncs progress and playlists across platforms, and provides search and support for audio and video podcasts.

Presentations

Android

Glogster [free] allows students using an Android-based device to create online multimedia posters, or Glogs, from a combination of media types (from audio, graphic, to video), and hyperlinks.

Google Slides [free] allows Android device users with a Google account a means of creating, editing, and collaborating with others on presentations.

LinkedIn SlideShare [free] allows Android device users the ability to search and explore for a variety of presentations, infographics, and documents on topics of their interest.

Microsoft PowerPoint [free] allows users to view PowerPoint presentations on their device for free, and to make edits and changes on the go.

iOS

Glogster [free] allows students using an iOS device to create online multimedia posters, or Glogs, from a combination of media types (from audio, graphic, to video), and hyperlinks.

Google Slides [free] allows iOS device users with a Google account a means of creating, editing, and collaborating with others on presentations.

Keynote [free] is a powerful presentation app that allows users to develop comprehensive presentations with animations, transitions, and multimedia elements.

LinkedIn SlideShare [free] allows iOS device users the ability to search and explore for a variety of presentations, infographics, and documents on topics of their interest.

Microsoft PowerPoint [free] allows users to view PowerPoint presentations on their device for free, and to make edits and changes on the go.

Computer

Microsoft PowerPoint [paid] is a comprehensive presentation software application, and is perhaps the most used and recognizable.

Keynote [free] is a powerful presentation app that allows users to develop comprehensive presentations with animations, transitions, and multimedia elements.

Web

Bunkr [free] is a presentation tool that displays any online content including social media posts, images, videos, audio, articles, and files.

Glogster [free] allows students to create online multimedia posters, or Glogs, from a combination of media types (from audio, graphic, to video), and hyperlinks.

Google Slides [free] allows those with a Google account, a means of creating, editing, and collaborating with others on presentations.

LinkedIn SlideShare [free] allows users to search for presentations, infographics, documents and other items on topics of their interest.

Microsoft PowerPoint Online [free] extends the Microsoft PowerPoint experience to the web browser with OneDrive integration, and allows users to create, edit, and view files on the go.

Prezi [free] is a visually oriented presentation packaged that also allows users to upload PowerPoint slides, and customize them, or use a variety of their own images, text, audio, and video.

Slidebean [free] offers a one-click presentation development system that incorporates a variety of templates into the design of presentations.

Slides [free] is a place for creating, presenting, and sharing slide decks.

Swipe [free] allows users to share a presentation link with anyone across any device, and it allows viewers to interact with the presentation on several levels, from collaboration through to taking polls.

VoiceThread [free] allows users to import various media such as images, PowerPoints, and PDFs. It provides a means of making audio or video recordings concerning those media artifacts, and it also allows other users to reply to the initial comments, by audio or video means, as the presentation progresses.

Publishing

Android

Book Creator Free [free] offers a simple means of creating a variety of ebooks including picture books, comic and photo books, and journals and textbooks. It allows for the use of images, narration, texts, annotations and drawings.

Book Writer Free [free] is a simple book creation application that allows users to share their content with others.

My Story Builder [free] is a simple, 'suitable for children', book editor.

Scribble: Kids Book Maker [paid] is an application that allows children to write, illustrate, and publish their own comprehensive stories in a range of formations including video export. It contains a series of story starters, stickers, and backgrounds to help them work on creating stories from the start.

iOS

Book Creator Free [free] offers a simple means of creating a variety of ebooks including picture books, comic and photo books, and journals and textbooks. It allows for the use of images, narration, texts, annotations and drawings.

Creative Book Builder [paid] is a professional ebook editor and generator which can also extend the utility of ebooks through the use of a range of widgets.

Demibooks Composer Pro [free] builds interactive books with animation, audio, images, and effects.

Scribble Press – Creative Book Maker for Kids [paid] contains a series of story starters, stickers and backgrounds to help get young kids working on creating stories that can be turned into ebooks.

Computer

Android Book App Maker [paid] provides users with the ability to turn content into a flip-book app.

iBooks Author [free] provides a series of templates and styles to assist in the development of ebooks for the iBook store.

Kotobee [free] provides free software to assist in the creation of ebooks and libraries for a range of platforms.

Web

Blurb [paid] is just one of many online services that can assist in the creation of ebooks.

QR Codes

Android

I-nigma QR & Barcode Scanner (free) is a versatile barcode and QR code reader that can scan a multitude of codes and share these codes as well.

QR Code Reader (free) is a simple QR Code and product barcode scanner.

QR Droid Code Scanner (free) is a powerful barcode, QR code, and Data Matrix scanner that offers multi-language support.

iOS

Bakodo – Barcode Scanner and QR Barcode Reader (free) scans all types of QR codes and barcodes.

QR Reader for iPhone (free) scans a variety of codes including QR codes and barcodes, and features auto-detect scanning.

QRafter – QR Code and Barcode Reader and Generator (free) is a two-dimensional barcode scanner for iOS. Along with a variety of useful features, it can scan and generate QR codes.

Computer

CodeTwo QR Code Desktop Reader (free) allows users to scan QR codes directly from their screen onto their desktop. Users select the QR code to be read by selecting the area with a QR code using their mouse.

QR-Code Studio (free) is for Mac and Windows computers. The QR code maker software is freeware.

Web

QR Code Generator (free) creates QR codes, in a limited number of formats, for free.

QR Stuff QR Code Generator (free) creates QR codes from a various types of data such as website URLs, image files, PDF files, and so on, with static and dynamic embedding options.

The QR Code Generator (free) allows for the free scan and generation of QR codes for a variety of uses.

Rubrics
Android

Daily Rubric: Any Curriculum [free] allows teachers to create and use rubrics from their Android device. Rubrics can be designed from curriculum outcomes, or based on the pre-loaded Common Core Standards.

iOS

Easy Assessment [paid] offers a means to capture and assess performance based on custom created rubrics, scale, or criteria.

Rubrics [paid] allows instructors to track student performance and produce reports based on custom rubrics and grading options.

Computer – n/a
Web

Kathy Shrock's Guide to Everything: Assessment and Rubrics [free] provides access to a wide range of rubrics to help guide assessment of students.

iRubric [free] is a website where instructors can create their own rubrics, or they can build off those made available from other instructors.

RubiStar [free] allows instructors to create their own rubrics using templates designed for core subjects as well as art, music, and multimedia.

Screencasting

Android

AZ Screen Recorder [free] is a screen recording application that offers several features, including the ability to capture the front camera as well as screen recording. It also provides video trimming.

ilos Screen Recorder [free] is a simple application that records the screen and provides audio capture as well.

Telecine [free] is an open source application that allows screen recording through the use of overlays.

iOS

Doceri [trial/paid] combines screencasting, desktop control, and an interactive whiteboard in one application, with control through Airplay or through Mac or PC.

Educreations Interactive Whiteboard [free] is an interactive whiteboard and screencasting tool that allows annotation, animation, and narration of a number of content types.

Screenchomp [free] allows users to annotate pictures or to use the application as a whiteboard. Any work completed with the application can be saved automatically to the internet.

Computer

ilos screen recorder [free] automatically uploads content to their servers for storage and playback.

Screencast-O-Matic [free] offers fifteen minutes of recording time for free, both for screen and webcam, and allows users to save to places such as YouTube or as a video file.

TechSmith Camtasia Studio [free trial] is a comprehensive screen recording application that allows for audio and webcam capture as well as highlighting, adding media, and editing of recordings.

Web – n/a

Storyboarding and Scripting

Android

Ray Story Board [free] is a simple storyboard creator that lets users build storyboards from photos or gallery images, create multiple storyboards, and animate them using a slideshow feature.

Storyboard Studio [paid] is a mobile storyboarding writing tool that is suitable for artists and non-artists alike.

iOS

Penultimate [free] provides a natural feel of writing and sketching on paper, and connects to Evernote.

Storyboard Composer [paid] is a mobile storyboard previsualiztion composer for animators, art directors, film students, film directors, or anyone who would like to visualize their story.

Computer

FrameForge Previz Studio [paid] allows users to develop and previsualize films, TV shows, commercials, or similar projects at a professional level.

Storyboardpro [paid] is professional level software that combines drawing and animation tools with camera controls.

StoryBoard Quick Studio [paid] allows for the fast creation of storyboards with QuickShots, has a print-to-sketch feature, and comes with a series of character poses for integration into storylines.

Web

Google Docs [free] can be used, along with any note-taking or document editor, as a make-shift storyboard by integrating photos or pictures into the document to outline a process or the actions for a story. It is also available as an Android and iOS app.

StoryboardThat [free trial] offers an edition that allows educators to build diagrams, and visualize workflow. It features a drag and drop interface and an extensive image library.

Story Creation Apps

Android

> *StoryMaker 1* [free] provides a means of creating stories using templates and overlays, and the possibility of using audio, photos, or video.

> *Storehouse* [free] allows users to share a collection of photos in a collage or album, or by telling a story that links the photos.

iOS

> *StoryKit* [free] allows for the creation of an electronic storybook through the use of images, simple drawings, recording of sound, and by the addition of text.

> *Storyrobe* [paid] makes photo-based slideshows with voice recording.

> *FotoBabble* [free] adds audio to a photo to make a talking postcard.

> *Sock Puppets* [free] lets users create lip-synced videos with characters. Various puppets, props, scenery, and backgrounds can be used.

Computer

Cartoon Story Maker 1.1 [free] is a simple program that creates 2D cartoon stories with conversations, dialogs (recorded and/or speech bubble), and various backgrounds.

StoryMaker [free/trial] is game-based software that asks for parts of speech (such as nouns, verbs, adjectives), and these are then inserted into a story with sometimes comical results. Educators can edit and customize aspects of the aspects of the program for their context. Backgrounds can be imported, but character templates are built in.

Web

Littlebirdtales [free] provides younger learners the ability to create digital storybooks.

Pixton [free/paid] is a visual writing tool that allows users to make a comic using images, clipart backgrounds and artwork, as well as speech bubbles.

Storynet.org [free] is a website that aims at connecting people to and through storytelling.

StoryJumper [free] allows users to create illustrated storybooks from scratch or from existing templates.

Video Editing

Android

VideoShow – Video Editor [free] is an all-in-one video editor and slideshow producer that provides music, themes, filters, emojis, as well as text input.

VidTrim [free] is a video editor and organizer that allows the trimming, editing, and saving of videos.

VivaVideo: Free Video Editor [free] is a comprehensive video editor and movie maker that facilitates the creation of video-based stories.

WeVideo [free] is a comprehensive and easy to use video editor that can mix images, text, video, and audio.

iOS

iMovie [paid] is video creation and editing software that can create easily shareable content.

Splice [free] is a video editor that adds music and effects to images and videos with narration. It includes access to free songs, sound effects, text overlays, transitions, filters, and various editing tools.

ReelDirector II [paid] is a full-featured video editing app.

WeVideo [free] is an easy to use and comprehensive video editor that can mix audio, images, text, and audio.

Computer

Windows Movie Maker [free] is a video editing software application that allows for narration, audio, images, and video to be mixed and edited with transitions and special effects.

Web

Video Toolbox [free] is an online video editing and conversion tool.

WeVideo [free] is a comprehensive and easy to use web-based video editor that can mix images, text, video, and audio together to form a compelling story.

Video Resources

Android

TED [free] provides more than 2,000 TED talks from various people by topic and mood, and on a variety of topics.

Vimeo [free] is a variety of videos are available across a wide variety of topics and genres, with users having the ability to upload their own content as well.

YouTube [free] allows for editing and uploading of videos, where one can subscribe to various channels that offer a wide variety of videos on various topics and genres.

iOS

TED [free] provides more than 2,000 TED talks from various people by topic and mood, and on a variety of topics.

Vimeo [free] provides a variety of videos which are available across a wide variety of topics and genres. Users are able to upload their own content as well.

YouTube [free] allows for editing and uploading of videos, where once can subscribe to various channels that offer a wide variety of videos on various topics and genres.

Computer – n/a

Web

Clipcanvas [free] allows for the download of 600,000 royalty free HD and 4K video and film clips.

Mazwai [free] maintains a collection of free to use HD video clips and footage, and some unique time-lapse and slow motion video footages that are provided under the Creative Commons Attribution license if used commercially.

Motion Backgrounds for Free [free] is a place to download professional quality motion backgrounds and video footage.

Motion Elements [free] is a good source for premium stock videos, offering around 400 videos for free, as well as free After Effects templates.

Neo's Clip Archive [free] offers nearly 3,500 free video clips sorted by 25 categories free for use for personal, non-commercial purposes.

Pexels Videos [free] brings under one roof a video library of Creative Commons Zero licensed stock videos from a variety of different sources.

SaveTube [free] allows users to rip YouTube videos to their local computer in various audio or video-based formats.

Savevideo.me [free] allows users to rip videos from a variety of sites to their local computer.

TeacherTube [free] is an online resource that helps users to view and share videos, photos, audio, and documents on almost any topic.

WebQuests

Android – n/a

iOS – n/a

Computer – n/a

Web

Building a WebQuest [free] is a comprehensive overview of the template to follow when there is a need to construct a WebQuest.

Having Fun with Reading [free] is a WebQuest for college and adult level learners of English, where learners interact with texts and complete activities that promote cooperative and collaborative learning along with reading narrative comprehension skills.

Idioms in Your Pocket [free] is a WebQuest that is designed for high school and adult ESL students, and it allows them to discover the various meanings of English idioms.

OneStopEnglish WebQuests [free] provides a selection of WebQuests covering major holidays.

Pre-Writing Your WebQuest [free] provides prompts for users to complete in order to develop a WebQuest.

QuestGarden [free/paid] is a site designed by Bernie Dodge, the creator of WebQuests, for use by pre- and in-service teachers, professional developers, other educators, and those who work with them. The site provides hosting and template creation of WebQuests that then become searchable.

Using WebQuests to Teach English [free] is a WebQuest that can be used to teach teachers about WebQuests.

WebQuestDirect [free] is described as the world's largest searchable directory of WebQuest reviews.

WebQuest.Org [free] provides comprehensive information pertaining to the WebQuest model, and is run by Bernie Dodge, the creator of WebQuests.

Zunal [free/paid] is a site for educators to create, host, and then share their WebQuests with others.

Wikis

Android

EveryWiki: Wikipedia++ [free] aims to provide access to many wikis from a central application.

wikiHow [free] is the application associated with the leading how-to-guide wikiHow. It allows for searching of the wiki to find step-by-step instructions on how to complete almost any task.

iOS

Hack My Life – Life Hack Wiki [free] is an application that seeks to provide access to all possible life hacks. A life hack is a strategy or technique that can be used or adopted to allow for better time management or for getting more out of everyday activities.

Lyrically [free] offers access to a list of song lyrics curated by fans. Searches can be undertaken by track, artist, or by song, and there is support for in-app purchases.

Computer

DokuWiki [free] is a PHP based highly customizable and fully extensible wiki software platform. The advantage is that it requires no databases as all the data is stored in plain text, and for this reason, it is very popular and used by many sites. It has a variety of useful features, from locking to avoid edits through to a spam blacklist.

MediaWiki [free] is open-source and it is the wiki software used by Wikipedia. It is available in a number of languages, released under a general public license (GPL), and written in PHP: Hypertext Preprocessor (PHP) a server-side scripting language. There are many extensions and plugins available for free, including a what-you-see-is-what-you-get (WYSIWYG) editor.

Web

PBworks [free] (formerly PBwiki) is a real-time collaborative editing system with several solutions including one for educators. It offers a single workspace, where student accounts can be created without email addresses, and easy editing without the need for coding.

PmWiki [free] is a wiki tool that gives user-access control over individual pages, so they can be set for access by specific people with it being possible to set different passwords for each page. The software also allows for navigation trails through individual sections, insertion of tables, and provides a printable layout.

Wikidot [free] offers members the ability to create a wiki-based website with forums, where they can create a community, or publish and share documents and content.

Wikispaces [free] is a wiki hosting service that provides educators with a means to monitor student progress in real time and the ability to easily create projects and assign them to students, as well as editing tools and a social newsfeed.

Teacher Notes

Android

_____

_____

_____

_____

_____

_____

_____

_____

_____

_____

_____

_____

_____

_____

_____

_____

_____

_____

_____

_____

_____

_____

_____

iOS

Computer

_____

_____

_____

_____

_____

_____

_____

_____

_____

_____

_____

_____

_____

_____

_____

_____

_____

_____

_____

_____

_____

Web

16
References

Bull, G., & Kajder, S. (2004). Digital storytelling in the language arts classroom. *Learning & Leading with Technology, 32*(4), 46-49.

Burden, K. & Atkinson, S. (2008). Evaluating pedagogical 'affordances' of media sharing Web 2.0 technologies: A case study. In Hello! Where are you in the landscape of educational technology? *ascilite, Melbourne, Australia.*

CDS. (2016). *Center for Digital Storytelling.* Retrieved from http://www.storycenter.org

Jakes, D. (2009). *Capturing stories, capturing lives: An introduction to digital storytelling.* Retrieved from http://www.jakesonline.org/dstory_ice.pdf

Jenkins, M., & Lonsdale, J. (2007). Evaluating the effectiveness of digital storytelling for student reflection. *ascilite, Singapore,* 440-444.

Lambert, J. (2010). *Digital storytelling cookbook.* Berkley, CA: Digital Diner Press.

Laurillard, D., Stratfold, M., Luckin, R., Plowman, L., & Taylor, J. (2000). Affordances for learning in a non-linear narrative medium. *Journal of Interactive Media in Education, 2.*

Martin, B. & Carle, E. (1995). *Brown bear, brown bear, what do you see?* Canada: Fitzhenry & Whiteside Ltd.

Ohler, J. B. (2008). *Digital storytelling in the classroom: New media pathways to literacy, learning, and creativity.* California: Corwin Press.

Robin, B. (2008). *The educational uses of digital storytelling - Getting started.* Retrieved from http://digitalstorytelling.coe.uh.edu/getting_started.html

Robin, B. (2016). *About digital storytelling.* Retrieved from http://digitalstorytelling.coe.uh.edu/page.cfm?id=27&cid=27&sublinkid=31

Robin, B. R., & Pierson, M. E. (2005). *A multilevel approach to using digital storytelling in the classroom.* Society for Information Technology & Teacher Education, Phoenix, AZ.

Schar, S., Schluep, S., Schierz, C., & Krueger, H. (2000). Interaction for computer aided learning. *Interactive Multimedia Electronic Journal of Computer-Enhanced Learning, 2(1)*.

About the Book

Digital storytelling clearly stands out as an exciting and captivating approach to use for both the teaching and practice of digital literacy, media literacy, and visual literacy skills. The exciting potential behind its use in the teaching of English to speakers of other languages (TESOL) is its ability to give a voice to those students who might come and sit quietly in class and rarely have a chance to speak. Success with digital stories therefore comes when students are empowered with the ability to talk about and make meaning from their life experiences. The pedagogical possibilities offered through the use of digital storytelling are presented while providing an overview of instructional strategies, tasks, and activities suitable for narrative development with second-language learners of English. Tutorials on how to get started with digital storytelling creation tools are included, along with photocopiable handouts and templates, evaluation techniques, and a comprehensive list of a wide variety of resources.

About the Author

David Kent is an Assistant Professor at the Graduate School of TESOL-MALL at Woosong University in the Republic of Korea. He has been working and teaching in Korea since 1995, and with a Doctorate of Education from Curtin University in Australia, he is a specialist in computer assisted language learning (CALL) and the teaching of English to speakers of other languages (TESOL). He has presented at international conferences, as well as published a number of peer-reviewed journal articles, books, and book chapters in his areas of specialization.

Also by David Kent

*A Loanword Approach to the Teaching of
English as a Foreign Language in Korea:*
Exploring the Effectiveness of a Multimedia Curriculum

TESOL Strategy Guides
Digital Storytelling
The Prezi Presentation Paradigm